But He Said He Was A Christian

But He Said He Was A Christian

Chayil Champion

Cosby Media Productions

Information:

info@cosbymediaproductions.com

 Second Edition, February 2016

ISBN-13: 978-0692637302 (Cosby Media Productions)

ISBN-10: 0692637303

Typeset by Cosby Media Productions

Published in the United States of America

Special Thanks to....

My LORD and Savior Jesus Christ for allowing me to write on this subject and supplying me with the wisdom and insight to shed light on such matters. I pray all are blessed who read this. GOD bless you and keep you.

TABLE OF CONTENTS

Introduction:

An Epistle of an Imperfect Man

I have fallen so many times trying to climb this hill of perfection; trying to become the quintessential man of GOD. With that said, the pages in this book are not to condemn nor judge anyone. I consider myself to be the least just as The Apostle Paul stated in his letters. I have made bad decisions in my life that have given the kingdom of Heaven some bad marketing and PR. I have played the hypocrite, the whoremonger, the player, the deceiver, womanizer, thief, liar, cheater, and even a murderer if you consider the abortions I consented in. And to think, I did all of this even after I accepted Christ as my savior. My convictions were so heavy on me that I contemplated suicide many times. So how can a man of this caliber even consider himself to be a man of GOD? It's almost like "why even try when you've done so much dirt?" That thought derives in your head when you begin to ponder the expectations and added pressure that people put on you when you begin to declare your Christianity. People begin to watch you closely. As a man, you're watched how you carry yourself by other men and women. People want to see what the big deal is about this Christianity thing because at the end of the day our actions and reactions become our testimony. If there is the slightest hint of hypocrisy, you will be mocked, judged, and in some cases even excommunicated.

I struggled with the idea of writing this book because of my failures as a man of GOD, particularly when it came to the areas of relationships. With a trail of broken hearts behind me, including my own, one would possibly think, "What audacity you have to write this book!" That's just it. There's no audacity at all. As a matter of fact, I shied away from the idea on several occasions. In my own perception of myself, I was not qualified to write this book. I'm not a relationship expert at all. I don't have a degree in Family & Marriage Counseling. On top of all that, I went through a divorce only after two years of marriage. I am not a delusional man. Traditional wisdom would have notified anyone that I am surely not sanctioned to write such a book. Then the LORD reminded me of a passage of scripture in 1ST Corinthians 1:27-28.

"But GOD has chosen the foolish things of the world

to put to shame the wise, and GOD has chosen the weak of the world to put to shame the things which are mighty; and the base things of the world and the things which are despised GOD has chosen..."

He then reminded me that there were many famous men in the bible who sinned greatly, but still loved HIM. Just so I wouldn't condone or justify my sins, the LORD reminded me that these men repented and worked constantly on abstaining from repetitive sins. From the Old Testament to the New Testament, the LORD showed me these men, their flaws, their repentance, and their theological testimony that followed. They were redeemed men, qualified to speak and write by the moving of GOD's spirit over their lives. Then the LORD encouraged me and revealed why I am allowed to write such a book. My flaws and failures would become mile markers that I could look back on and see where I went wrong in my life. They would be used to help others from becoming victims of the same pitfalls. He assured me that I was redeemed because he saw my commitment to walk righteously before him and that my failures humbled me to a point where he could trust me to be transparent to those who would read my work.

In lieu of my bible geek nature, the LORD helped me tap into the word of knowledge according to the spiritual gifts that he put within me (1st Corinthians 12) to grasp an understanding behind the transgressions of men throughout biblical history. Through the LORD's wisdom, I have been able to correlate the struggles of men in the 21st century with the fall of man in the Garden of Eden. In addition, through my experiences and my walk with the LORD I have arrived at several conclusions on how we, men, can better ourselves and other men around us through accountability. I came to these resolves by understanding that the success of our relationship with the women in our life, our children, and even each other begin with us accepting the salvation of GOD and then *working* on that salvation daily with other men and women who teach us and edify us.

Many of us men have let down women through various forms of emasculation. We have lied to them. We have cheated on them. We have blamed them for issues in our life that they have nothing to do with. We have used double-standards against them to justify our actions and disqualify theirs. We have promised them many changes that we would make only to remain the same. We have been inconsistent with our women. They need more from us. In addition, we have let down the entire world. Romans 8:19 reminds us that all of creation is waiting for the sons of GOD to be revealed. Unfortunately, many of us have delayed our revealing because we haven't given the world anything to see other than a bunch of broken promises. Because we call ourselves men of GOD, the expectation of us is held to a higher standard. It is safe to say that if you are willing to call yourself a Christian or a man of GOD, the bar has been raised. This is not to say that people should be putting their trust in man in the first place. We all should be putting our trust in the LORD who will guide our steps and lead us in all righteousness. However, this does not let men of GOD off the hook when it comes to walking in loyalty, devotion, trust, boldness, decisiveness, virtue, integrity, and love above all things. There is an expectation that we are called to.

Anew, these pages are not to condemn men or blame us of the horrible way we've treated women over time, collectively. Instead, the folios of this book are to challenge a good number of men, including myself to truly transform into the men of GOD we were called to be. Another objective is to give women insight on why we experience many hurdles in our relationships with each other spiritually, emotionally, intimately and platonically. I pray that this doctrine will trigger men and women to look closer at the GOD who created us and turn to HIM to improve our roles as men and women of GOD; subsequently allowing us to model admirable, righteous relationships in our marriages and courtship in the sight of others who have their eyes on us. In this, we pray they might see the testimony and work of GOD in all of us. Amen.

Chapter 1:

The Garden's Domestic Dispute

I had a friend tell me once that she was done dating men inside the church. I asked her why and she answered that men in the church were just as trifling, if not more, as men who didn't go to church. She said she didn't see the difference between a Christian man and a worldly man. It turns out that she had been dating a man who was heavily involved in ministry at their church. He was an usher, served on various church committees, and even served as a youth minister for their teen ministry. Though he showed himself to be a man of GOD, he struggled with flirting. He would even entertain taking other women out for "coffee" or "lunch" and justify it as "counseling" because "they were going through something." Then she caught him having dinner at a restaurant outside of their local community; it was with one of her best friends. This was after he told her he had to work late. She, taking the time for a girls' night out with her friends, happened to choose the same restaurant which was many miles away from their respective, usual hangouts. You could probably imagine the awkwardness of that situation when they both saw each other; his embarrassment coupled with her hurt and disdain. It was over for them obviously, but it was the start of much pain for her accompanied by a new distrust of men in the church.

Her struggle to heal over the "church" hurt that she had been experiencing had much to do with a perception that compartmentalizes and distinguishes people of faith compared to people who are of a secular state of mind. She failed to realize that people of faith struggle and fall to fleshly temptation. We all tend to forget that all of us were born in sin and have to be delivered from a worldly mindset. Our decisions to follow Christ don't exempt us from making dumb mistakes, though over time we are expected to mature into righteousness. A man or women's faith in the LORD does not make them above reproach to sin. I speak collectively. Her hurt was deep due to the expectation that people have of those who call themselves Christian. The expectation that a woman has of her man to be faithful and loyal becomes scorned the moment he deceives her. Now you have a heart that was once willing to love marred by disdain with the inability to trust again.

So how do we handle this taboo topic of dating and intimacy in the church that sometimes causes confusion and hurt? Let us first deal with the blurry perception people have of Christians in general. As it pertains to relationships, even some of the most astute men of the bible failed to honor GOD and their wives under the proper context of marriage. Men like Abraham, Jacob, Sampson, David, and Solomon were just a few of the men who struggled with monogamy.

These were all men of GOD and I'm sure without a doubt that the women in the community despised their doggish ways when their misdeeds became public. Sarah showed her disdain for Abraham sleeping with Hagar. It didn't matter that they both agreed on it for the "purpose" of conception. It was wrong, and Abraham being a man, acted on his fleshly lusts. The act of sex starts with some type of attraction, whether it be misguided or under the proper context of marriage. Though his sin was not justified, Hagar was young and beautiful and Sarah was old. Abraham, through his wife's approval, took a free pass to sin. His motives were not totally focused on assisting GOD with his plan to make him a father of many nations. Trust me! There was a lust and a desire already dwelling within him to sleep with Hagar. GOD's charge to Abraham in Genesis chapter 17 was a charge for Abraham to sin no more and to walk perfectly. HE was speaking to his infidelity and purity issues among other idiosyncratic flaws.

As for the other men; Jacob conceived children by three other women before having children with the wife he had initially asked for in Rachel. According to Judges Chapter 16, Sampson had sex with a harlot on his way to Gaza. David committed adultery with Bathsheba while she was married to Uriah (2nd Samuel 12) and finally Solomon, David's son, was lured away from righteousness by his love for multiple women (1st Kings 11:1-8). We have to get to a point of understanding that no one person is above reproach when it comes to sin. My friend allowed her hurt to dictate her perception of Christian men based upon her expectation.

On the flip side, as a men's ministry leader, I have heard men ask, "Why was it okay for men to have more than one wife in the early history of the bible compared to now?" The answer is that it was *NEVER* okay! The desire to have more than one wife was due to greed that developed inside of mankind once sin became present after the fall of Adam and Eve in the Garden of Eden. Genesis chapter 6 sheds light on the multiplication of ungodly men throughout the earth. The first thing that the word of GOD addresses in the chapter was the lust of men.

Genesis 6: 1-2,5~ "And it came to pass, when men began to multiply on the face of the earth, and daughters were born to them, that the sons of GOD saw the daughters of men as beautiful; and they took many wives for themselves... And GOD saw that the wickedness of man was great in the earth, and that every imagination of the thoughts of his heart was evil continually."

A good percentage of men in the church don't even know where the origin of their struggle comes from when it comes to objectifying women. Some attribute it to generational strongholds, peer pressure, cultural conditioning, or even from being hurt due to previous relationships. These are all foundational cornerstones which breed unfaithfulness, but for us men to know the root of our failure when it comes to relationships we must fully grasp what happened in Eden during the fall of man.

Adam and Eve's relationship in the garden was more than just a tale of the first husband and wife team. It was the model of a perfect relationship between man and woman. Their union with GOD and their union with each other was a spiritual DNA strand, which when it was merged with sin, created relational catastrophe for all of us. The Garden of Eden was predicated on multiple relationships. First there was a perfect relationship with man and GOD, which was the foundation of peace in all relationships. Then there was a perfect relationship with man and nature; man and beasts, and then there was a relationship with man and woman. All of these relationships hinged upon the relationship between man and GOD. Once the relationship between man and GOD went south, so would all the other relationships. GOD had established

Shalom, perfect peace, with all creation. There was no turmoil, dissension, catastrophe, or disagreements among any of GOD's creations. Everyone and everything were in unison.

However, when Adam and Eve allowed sin to enter into their lives through disobedience, division became present in every relationship; GOD and man, man and nature, and in the context of marriage, man and woman's relationship became equally tumultuous. There was now a domestic dispute between Adam and Eve. The oneness that Adam had with his wife was now severed. As the LORD confronted Adam on his role as an accomplice to sin, Adam began to place the blame on Eve.

> "That woman, whom you gave me to be with, she gave me the fruit from the tree and I ate," replied Adam

(Genesis 3:12).

Adam's perception of his wife had now changed. The consequential effect would now permeate throughout history collectively. Relationally, the two genders would strive forever from that time to now. Understand, prior to sin, Adam and Eve had a perfect marriage. Adam was her covering and Eve was his helpmate. They lived harmoniously, free of dispute, and there was joy and satisfaction with each other. As the LORD handed down the dreadful sentence that would affect mankind for eternity, Adam never regarded Eve in the same light and she never saw her husband the same either. The joy and satisfaction they once had with one another would now share the space with misery and "you make me sick!"

Think about it for a moment. You're walking with GOD...in person. You visibly can see him and you two are very close. Eternal life is the palm of your hands and you live in a paradise setting. Then, in a moments time you are banned from paradise, told you are going to die, and you lose your relationship with your best friend all because you and your spouse participated in a crime. Yes, I can see the "it's your fault" arguments happening instantaneously. This is not to suggest that Adam never loved Eve again or that they didn't apologize to each other, but their decision to sin cut off the source of all relationships; the Father's, and this ultimately left them to deal with each other under a new dichotomy filled with sin.

Adam and Eve's sentencing had so many intrinsic ramifications on the intimate relationship that takes place between a man and woman even now well into the 21st century. Many of us in our humanity or apathy would overlook these implications as diminutive. The perfect social order of relationships between man and woman was disrupted on so many levels; beginning with the way we communicate all the way to understanding the needs and roles of one another. The patience that man was to have for his wife was affected as well as his commitment to monogamy. The sin of men and women carry generational outcomes on those born later. Adam and Eve didn't see their sin causing a riff in their relationship, nor did they see the domino effect it would have in the relationships of other men and women throughout time. In general, man and woman would not have the harmonious relationship that GOD intended for us. Even the equality that women fight for among men today was cut off in the Garden.

Genesis 3:16 "To the woman GOD said: 'I will greatly multiply your sorrow and your conception; in pain you shall bring forth children; your desire shall be for your husband, and he shall rule over you."

Though the LORD was speaking directly to Adam and Eve, he was also speaking to the generations of us who would come to understand his Word. I'm not implying that men and women can never have great relationships in marriage, dating, or even on a platonic level. However, the intentional, perfect peace that man was to have with woman was lost that day in the Garden of Eden. The only relationships that are built on firm foundations are the ones that are truly built on the word of GOD with Christ at the center. I'm not talking about the relationships of couples who call themselves "Christians". That's just a title alone. I'm talking about the couple who seek the LORD together while supporting each other's mission in their kingdom calling. If we distinguished ourselves by titles alone, we would find more Christian divorced couples than those who do not declare themselves Christians.

There are, indeed, couples who have great relationships who are not in Christ. On the same note, there are couples in Christ who struggle within the confines of their unity. The mystery behind that enigma rests on the grace of GOD. Hurdles arise in any relationship, whether it be rocky or firm. At the end of the day, true solace can only be found on the principles of GOD who is the source of our relationships with each other. If we are disconnected from the main source who is supposed to be our primary relationship, then any other relationship we try to build is at risk of failure whether it be intimate or platonic. Here is where I put the onus on us men to reassume our positions in this world as kingdom-minded men who truly follow GOD. The imbalance of the world began with our ineptitude to obey GOD and consult with him regularly. The restoration of the world rests on us beginning to seek GOD continually. Until men claim the responsibility of rightfully restructuring their relationship with the LORD, generally speaking, the women will continually find fault with us and we will struggle to understand their needs causing conflict in our rapport with each other.

Chapter 2:

Genesis 6: The Evil, Infidelity, and Greed of Man

Not all men are dogs, but all men have the propensity to cheat inside of them. I love the look on a woman's face after I respond to her questions, "why do men cheat?" or "why can't men make up their minds and decide what they want?" These questions are frequently asked by women to other men because they want to get an idea of what is going on our minds; particularly when there is drama in the relationship. I tend to respond with one phrase; "Genesis 6." I usually get a "huh?" with a raised eyebrow. After I stop laughing at their bemusement, I do take the time to explain that man's flaws can be attributed directly to something that took place in the family generation line. Some people would even say that the way a man treats a woman is based upon the way he was conditioned or who he saw as the models of man-woman relationships during the days of his adolescence. These are true among other factors, but I also tie in the evil that began to settle in the hearts of man in Genesis 6.

In chapter 1, I referenced Genesis 6 as the chapter where sin multiplied upon the face of the earth. It was also the chapter where GOD sheds light on the greed inside of the hearts of men prior to the flood. Now, we all know that sin was already present on the face of the earth because of the events that took place with Adam and Eve. When we journey through the next few chapters we see the first murder when Cain slew his brother Abel *(Genesis 4).* They were the sons of Adam and Eve. The premise behind the murder was anger and jealousy which were preludes to sin. In lieu of his transgression, Cain would go on to be the legacy-starter of an ungodly generation. The LORD would give Adam and Eve another son through their conception named Seth. Seth would produce a godly generation. To distinguish the two is necessary before we begin to chase the origins of men's promiscuity.

In Genesis chapter 4, we learn of a man named Lamech who was the great, great, great-grandson of Cain. He is the first account of a man taking two wives. Remember, that his great grandfather Cain committed murder and would, in turn, produce ungodly seeds in his family line. As I mentioned earlier, it was never intended for man to have more than one wife nor was it ever okay with GOD. Lamech also committed murder as did Cain *(Genesis 23).* Cain's generational line would continue to breed men with deceitful hearts that would eventually lead to the wickedness and judgment of man that we read about when we get to Genesis 6.

Prior to the flood and the account of Noah, the scriptures speak about a group of men who were descendants of Cain that become ensnared by the beauty of women. Because of the sinful nature that continued in the legacy of Cain's generational line, the willingness to sin grew exceedingly. This was a spiritual, generational stronghold that spread rapidly because of a lack of godliness among the men. None of these men were taught to live righteously. So, just like their relative predecessor, Lamech, these men took on multiple wives to fulfil their desires. Because they were separate from the righteousness of GOD, the beauty of one woman was not enough for them. Genesis 6:2 states that “they took wives for themselves of all whom they chose.” This means that many of them took more than one wife. They saw women as property and the men took it upon themselves to step outside the confines of marriage that GOD had created. Man had become greedy, taking excessively more than what he was allotted under the principles of GOD. The rest of the verses in chapter 6 tell us how the LORD was grieved that he had even created man because the “thoughts of man’s heart was evil continually.” *(Genesis 6:5-6)*

The flood initially was meant to wipe out these ungodly men from the face of the earth. The LORD’s plan was to preserve the godly line of men and women through Noah and his family. The Ark that Noah built in Genesis 6, was to keep him and his family safe. Looking through the eyes of the Spirit, one could say it was a protective capsule for righteousness as the storm would destroy all that was unrighteous. Noah was a man who walked upright in the sight of the LORD. It was Noah’s righteousness that moved the LORD to re-establish his covenant with man through Noah. So what is the correlation between this account and the manner of men towards women?

The nature of sin is constantly within man. Noah and his son Ham proved this. Noah allowed sin to enter into his family line. As GOD's conduit, who was supposed to reinitiate the human race with righteousness, Noah became drunk after the flood subsided as he drank excessively from his wine produced by the grapes in his vineyard (Genesis 9). Through his drunkenness, he undressed himself and fell asleep. Noah's youngest son, Ham, acted out of immaturity and instead of covering his father he went to tell his brothers. This caused Noah to curse his son out of anger, which led to another blemished generational line. Much like the event of Cain, Ham would also breed an ungodly generational line. Ham's son, Canaan, was the father of the Canaanites who actually inhabited Sodom and Gomorrah where the sin became so great that GOD had to destroy the place. The same pattern of immorality began with men taking on many wives and then even turning to themselves as lovers (Genesis 18 &19). Once again, men had lost their place with the LORD. From that point until now, the righteousness of man has had to contend with sin.

Men have struggled to walk righteously with GOD since the beginning of time and it has affected our ability to be content. The sins of men that occurred pre-flood and post flood stemmed from discontentment. They were not satisfied with what GOD had given them, so they took more until they felt their desires were fulfilled. This included everything from food to money, power, possessions, and women. Sadly enough, the men of the 21st century wrestle with the same spiritual diseases that plagued men during the time of both Cain and Ham. Greed, sexual immorality, and lust after worldly possessions are just a few of the common moral ailments that have plagued men over the centuries because we were discontent with the guidelines and restrictions that GOD issued to us for our safety. Over time, we have allowed the evils into our homes, families, marriages and churches. The infestation of our mutating transgressions along with pride has caused men to become distant in their relationship with GOD, hence making it difficult for man to be content with anything including our women.

The Pentecostal Pimp: Walking The Dogs

Much like my friend, many women in the church are let down by men because of their expectation that comes along with the title “Christian man.” The church as a whole has done a terrible job of discipleship when it comes to training men how to walk in their kingdom identity let alone monogamy. So often, because of the lack of sound discipleship, men in the church are operating out the “milk” of the word and not the “meat” (1st Corinthians 3:2 & Hebrews 5:12). Overall, we haven’t grown up enough in the WORD of GOD, so the bad habits that we bring in from the world remain with us when we walk into the church. Then we begin to exercise those bad habits, which ultimately gives the identity of the “Christian” a bad reputation according to the world’s perspective. Then we hear remarks like, “You’re worse than I am! I thought you were a Christian!” To my experience and witnessing, many young men in the church endure the humbling conviction when they learn they are behaving contrary to GOD’s word. Carrying a worldly and fleshly disposition, many single men walk in the church with the intent to seek the LORD, but end up distracted by the beauty of the women in the pews. Reminiscent of the men of Genesis 6, some of the men become subject to seeing how many girls they can get within the church to satisfy their fleshly desires. Oblivious to their sinful nature, they begin to attach "leashes" to the hearts of multiple women in the congregation.

What we have to recognize is this; all of us were born into sin regardless of our generational line. Just because we attach a label to our name doesn't change who we are. Only the LORD is able to transform us and he does it the more we seek him out. All of us have partnered with the world to some degree before coming to Christ. So when someone walks into the church for the first time as many of us have, they are walking in with the same filth of sin from the world attached to them that we all have been trying to shed off. Now, there is an expectation and a charge that comes from GOD as we grow in our Christian walk. We are expected to mature from our worldly ways as we walk with Christ. Sometimes, there is a delay in that maturation process because our men lack the *discipline* that only comes with *discipleship and mentoring*. If a man who was a "player" or a whoremonger walks into church with the intention to give his life to Christ, much of his success in transformation will hinge on; 1. His desire to truly seek the LORD on his own will, and 2. The level of discipleship and teaching taking place at that particular house of worship. Each man's maturation process is different. We lose sight of this as do many of the women in the congregation. In addition, many of the young women in the church are still going through a maturation process themselves. When a man of GOD who hasn't fully matured connects with a woman in the church who hasn't fully matured, there is usually an inevitable mess that occurs in the days or months following.

Though I am not a female, I understood my female friend's frustration with us men. In the men's group that I led for two years, I recognized the many relational issues that men struggled with when it came to the opposite sex. The age group of the men I led were between 22 and 40. Many were new in their walk with Christ. A good handful had accepted the LORD as their savior, but they hadn't been exposed to sound discipleship. As I got to know them, I noticed that a lot of the younger men were forming inappropriate relationships with the women of the church. In their hopes of "finding a wife" they were entertaining multiple dating opportunities with women in the congregation.

The outcome was woeful. Many women who were friends became enemies after finding out they were dating the same guy. I saw women who were trying to grow close to GOD, fall away because they were church hurt by the men who deceived them. I saw men, unaware of their own distraction, coming to church to hear a message only to have it go in one ear and out the other as they continued their covert attempts to court women. They hoped that no one saw their true colors.

The men were "walking the dogs" as I call it. They were spiritually attaching leashes to the hearts of multiple women hoping that they would find "the one" most suitable for them. Some engaged in premarital sex, which complicated things even further. What these men didn't realize is that those leashes had a double-end neck noose...or heart noose for that matter. Now they found themselves being walked like a dog-walker; walking multiple dogs bigger and stronger than them.

The hearts of these men were being pulled in different directions. They found it hard to let go of the women they were seeing. I saw other men of GOD objectifying women as if they were their property. In the process, some of the men became jealous of each other when they found out they were going after the same type of women. At the same time, many of the women were playing the same games as the men. In their search for "Mr. Right", some women allowed themselves to be courted by as many men as they thought liked them. Sometimes it was for a free meal. As I spoke to other friends of mine who were leaders in churches around the country, they concurred that the same nonsense was happening in their congregations as well.

The young men were more interested in finding a wife than finding truth. Unaligned with the WORD of GOD, too many men incur the title as a "Pentecostal pimp" because they're pursuing love in the wrong measures and context. Sound discipleship would teach these men not to seek a wife (1st Corinthians 7:27). Instead, these men would learn how to seek things above (Colossians 3:1) as their lives are hidden in Christ. Our lives being hidden in Christ means that everything in our life is hidden in HIM, including our marriages, finances, education, etc. However, even as we learn this through scripture, it takes more than us simply coming into agreement with GOD's word. We have to live it and that means breaking off bad habits that we picked up before we came to know Christ.

Many of us men fail to recognize the responsibility and expectation that are tacked on to us when we let others know that we are a Christian. As cliché as the title has become to society, it still carries a degree of weight for those of us who take it seriously. Before we can become a husband or a mate to any woman, we have to make sure we are walking in the fullness of our calling in Christ. Some of us mature in our knowledge of Christ, but sometimes we can take a long time to develop in certain areas of our life. In addition to that, we must maintain our righteousness in the areas that we have matured in. For instance, a man who struggled with sexual purity before he came to know the LORD has to maintain his spiritual disciplines in order to not fall back into the same temptations. If we are not careful, we can find ourselves falling to the same temptations that we at one time overcame. This requires a lot of work which include reading, prayer, worship, and fellowship on a consistent basis. Paul reminds us in Galatians 5 that the flesh and the Spirit war with one another. If we allow our flesh to have victory over us in any sense, then we become susceptible to sin. We guard ourselves against sin by consistently consulting with GOD daily. Listening to a message from a pastor on Sunday is not enough and many of us men have missed our mark because we have reduced our salvation to just that; hearing a sermon and then leaving like we haven't learned anything.

There is so much more that we are called to. Men have to recognize that salvation is a work. This is why Paul charged us along with the church of Philippi to "work out our salvation with fear and trembling" (Philippians 2:12). The fear that Paul is referring to is the reverence that we have for GOD. When we treat women like property and toy with their hearts we show that we don't have a proper fear of the LORD. It means that we haven't truly learned what it means to fear GOD. Having a respect for GOD and fearing GOD are two different things. Not enough men have learned the difference, which allows certain males to feel like they are doing nothing wrong when they begin "searching for their wife." This often makes us look like the dogs that many women ascribe some of us to be. A man who respects GOD, knows that there is a GOD and may even attend church time to time out of that respect. A man who fears GOD, reads his WORD daily and through much prayer and meditation allows the LORD to direct his steps every day of the week. Sundays are simply days of reaffirmation to the man who fears GOD. The man who respects GOD but doesn't fear HIM, allows his church affiliation to dictate his title and identity without knowing the full measure of responsibility that he carries.

In order for the Pentecostal pimp to become the devoted deacon, he must adhere to EVERY word of GOD and make the LORD his primary chase for a relationship. It is indeed a discipline that is easier said than done because it is established on the pillars of trusting beyond what we can see. Through his pursuit of GOD, he will come to into the knowledge of understanding that he is called to lead and cover, but the woman that GOD places in his life when he finally matures will be there as his equal to support him.

Chapter 3:

When A Proverbs 31 Woman meets a Psalm 112 Man

Lately, I have heard some men say that they want a Proverbs 31 woman. When we study the context of that scripture, we see several attributes that would have all of us men wanting a woman of that caliber. We see a woman who is loyal and trusted by her husband (v11); a woman who is resourceful (v13 & v14); she is diligent and not lazy (v15); she runs her own business (v24); she's intelligent and wise (v26) she keeps the house beautiful and in order (v22 &v27), and above all she FEARS the LORD (v30). As men, we often complain through our double-standard*ish* ways in desire of such a woman. We blame the women that we're with for faults that really have nothing to do with them when we become frustrated. Often, we emasculate our woman when we see there are attributes absent that we wanted or hoped for within them. On the other hand, hardly do we ever think of what the desire is of the woman concerning her man.

A woman who fears the LORD wants a man who fears the LORD as well. Some women have even gone as far as trying to convince their boyfriends or husbands to come to church with them in hopes that the pastor's words would change their men into God-fearing vessels. There is nothing wrong with desiring salvation for another person. We ought to want everyone to get saved but in the proper context. Desiring salvation for a man or a woman because we're dating them or want to date them is an improper motive. There is no such thing as a quick fix in the Kingdom of GOD. The fear of the LORD has to come through a desire to seek and know HIM. A man of GOD is molded by the hands of the LORD through chastening, teaching, longsuffering, prayer, and studying the word of GOD. Walking a man into a church building banking on immediate change, will only result disappointment. The process of GOD's time has to be factored in and none of us have the precise timeframe for that. Women and men desiring to be in a relationship have to develop the patience to wait on GOD. Most men who cry out for a Proverbs 31 woman hardly have developed into the men of GOD that they were called to be. Women in the church pushing for a man to become redeemed so she can date him is a woman who hasn't allowed herself to be completely filled by GOD's love.

Proverbs 31 describes what a complete woman who fears the LORD looks like. The scripture listed the spiritual and internal attributes of a woman of GOD. The book of Proverbs doesn't provide such a description for a man, though there are many scriptures that tell the story of great men who loved the LORD. However, one passage of scripture describes the essence of a righteous man much like Proverbs 31 spoke about the virtuous woman. With the similar uses of the "he" and "she" pronouns in the two chapters, the writer of the both passages sound like they could be the same author. The man described in Psalm 112 sounds like the perfect match for the Proverbs 31 woman. As we look at this man of GOD, which all men are capable of becoming, we can see the parallels between he and his female counterpart described in Proverbs 31; The Psalm 112 man fears the LORD (v1); his generations will be upright and mighty on the earth because of his legacy (v2); wealth and riches will be in his house because of his diligence and trust in the

LORD (v3); his righteousness is continuous, not sporadic (v3); he is gracious and full of compassion (v4); he lends to those in need (v5); he keeps his business quiet and governs with wisdom (v5); He is not afraid of evil (v7); His heart steadily trusts in the LORD without wavering (v7 & v8); he gives to the poor (v9). You don't have to read too far to see that the Proverbs 31 woman and the Psalm 112 man have essential attributes in common.

The husband of the woman of GOD in Proverbs 31 is mentioned three times during the discourse of her description. In the short depiction we get of him we can infer that he is a godly man with some of the attributes mentioned in Psalm 112. The loyalty between he and his wife established a trust, making his faithfulness transparent (Proverbs 31:11). The man of GOD described in Psalm 112 and the virtuous woman in Proverbs 31 are attainable and when the man and woman mature into these godly roles as individuals. It makes for a wonderful union when the LORD brings them together, but it is their patience in GOD and recognition of the change in each other that allows HIM to qualify their union.

The issue, once again, is that many men are not taught how to become the godly men that we are charged to be. Our role models have become scarce and many of us who have the opportunity to change the cycle often find ourselves contributing to the perpetual failure of mis-educating others with bad doctrine and examples. Even now, there is a major disparity in the ratio of women to men who faithfully serve the LORD. My perception of the role and definition of a man of GOD is he that is a servant-leader who ministers to the physical and spiritual needs of the church and the surrounding communities. However, the young men in our generation are struggling to grasp an understanding of the intimacy that we must have with the LORD to mature into such a man. Therefore, there is a large amount of men missing from the arena of servanthood, which is critical when it comes to a marriage or a relationship. A lot of it has to do with pride. Pride keeps us from fearing the LORD properly, which is the first attribute mentioned in Psalm 112. We're all guilty of pride. We have all been consumed at one time or another by the "all about me-mentality". I must admit, I'm probably a bit more exposed to it having lived in Los Angeles for the past several years of my life. I'm still somewhat amazed when I walk in church and see men jockeying for positions, looking for notoriety, trying to establish themselves as important, and disregarding the service of the sanctuary all together. Once again, I speak in general terms, but the number of men truly answering the call of the LORD are slight compared to the number of men who aren't. The underlying reason behind this disparity is that a great percentage of men alive today are not spirit-led. Too many of us are led by the world's standards and trends. The chase for money captivates many of us; yes, even a large number of us in the church. We want to be seen, heard, and respected on every platform. Without even giving notice to it, our pride has made us a stench to GOD.

Pride has been the fall of many pastors. I recall sitting in one of the larger churches in South Florida and hearing a very prominent pastor at the time, reveal to his congregation that he was leaving his wife for another woman. Prior to that, one of the assistant pastors of a church I was attending in Miami, left his family because he had grown bored of his wife and convinced himself that he was in love with another woman. I remember how hurt the congregation was when our senior pastor announced the travesty. At the time, I wondered how men of GOD could fall to such low standards only to find myself years later at the center of divorce and separation from my family because of promiscuous acts that I committed. It was through that shame that GOD taught me that we have to maintain a continuous walk in the Spirit at all times. The moment we step out, we become susceptible to wicked thoughts, evil desires, discontentment, and sinful deeds. In addition, pride will consume us and have us thinking that we are right in our own eyes when we are clearly wrong. A lot of us men even justify our transgression through pride by coming up with our own theories and philosophies. We disregard scripture and instead come up with our own rules that fit us making our doctrine faulty at best. Paul warned about this in the book of Galatians.

When we are not walking in the Spirit it means we no longer have the mind of Christ that Paul perfectly describes in 1st Corinthians 2. A Psalm 112 man knows how to walk according to the fruits of the Spirit referenced in Galatians 5. As Paul was addressing the church in Galatia he was addressing men and women who allowed the gospel of Christ to escape their hearts. They had become bewitched by false teachers and false doctrine. We become impressionable to such delusions when we are complacent in seeking the truth of GOD. The world's standards become the ruler by which we measure ourselves. Our pride won't allow us to receive correction or reproof because we become offensive while thinking others our judging us. However, Paul reminds us in his letter to Galatia, that if we walk according to the fruits of the Spirit, we won't become subjected to the lust of flesh (Galatians 5:16).

The fruits of the Spirit, according to Galatians 5:22-23, are love, joy, peace, longsuffering, kindness, goodness, faithfulness, gentleness, and self-control. Out of the nine fruits, I've seen men struggle the most with longsuffering (patience during trials) and with self-control. These are two essential characteristics in order for us to succeed in our relationships with women. More so, we need to operate from them as we progress in our relationship with the LORD. When we push the LORD to the side and begin trying to live life on our own, we lose...well...control of our self-control and we lose our patience. When we lose our patience, our tolerance level takes a dip and we often find ourselves frustrated. Self-control in Christ means not giving into the temptation. When we're not walking in the fruits of the Spirit, self-control is absent which means we'll give in to any urge. When I thought about all the men who fell to temptation, including myself, I discovered that all of us were void of one common fruit; that being self-control. We were working according to the flesh. When the Spirit is not in control, the flesh goes haywire!

The LORD charges us to walk in the Spirit, so we won't lose self-control and start feeding our flesh the garbage it desires. What does the flesh desire? The flesh desires adultery (women outside of our marriage), fornication (sex outside of marriage), idolatry (worldly possessions), selfish-ambitions (gain for yourself), drunkenness (liquor, drugs that numb the senses and emotions), and revelries (wild parties, clubs, orgies). These are few of the fleshly desires that men succumb to according to Galatians 5:19-21. It doesn't matter if you call yourself a Christian or not, all men are not above reproach when it comes to these.

Any and everybody can lose themselves to these fleshly desires whether you're a priest, pastor, bishop, or a deacon. All it takes is a few moments of distraction, taking your eyes off the LORD and your flesh will be setting your heart, mind, soul, and your body up for the fall. This is why Jesus tells us to love the LORD with all our "heart, soul, and mind." Our love for the LORD is the only thing powerful enough to maintain our walk in the Spirit, but a lack of humility keep many of us men from loving the LORD in the fullness of the "heart, soul, and mind" capacity.

Humility vs. Pride: Man's Battle within Himself

The biggest battle the majority of us men have is with pride and if there is one thing that continually pulls us from Spirit back to flesh, this would be it.

Pride is the element that keeps men from developing the intimate relationship that GOD requires from us. Men mistakenly view intimacy in the wrong context making it hard for many of us to connect with GOD on a deeper level. When pride distorts our perception of intimacy with the LORD, it also distorts our perception of intimacy with our wives or potential mates. Simply put, pride causes us to sin.

Picture King David standing upon the roof of his palace as the chapter opens in 2nd Samuel 11. He is supposed to be in battle, but uses his authority to remain in the comforts of his home. As he stands on the roof he sees a very beautiful woman bathing. He sends someone to go inquire about her and finds out that she is married. Earlier, I mentioned how the men of this present time sometimes come in to the sanctuary and become distracted by the women. Their intention to come seek GOD gets sidetracked by a desire to find companionship with certain women of the church. David was a man who loved the LORD fully, and when he saw Bathsheba bathing he allowed his fleshly desire to overtake his focus in the Spirit. Here it is, a godly man is now operating outside of his kingdom identity, because his pride told him that he could have Bathsheba because of his position. It was a mistake that would change his life in many aspects.

David decides to take Bathsheba against all

righteousness and sleeps with her. She becomes pregnant and David tries to cover up the act by conspiring to have her husband killed, which happened eventually. At the end of the chapter, we are reminded that David's acts displeased the LORD. The LORD saw David's issue deeper than the acts of sin he committed. David had to pay a pretty steep price for sins, but the LORD knew that it was necessary in order to humble David. The LORD despises pride and many of us men wreak of it.

A large number of us men were conditioned to be bold, show no fear, don't cry, don't show emotion, don't let anyone punk you and don't be sensitive. Many of us learned this in our childhood depending on who we looked up to. Some of us who didn't have dads growing up, learned how to handle ourselves and how to handle women from what the streets taught us. It was the wrong curriculum and sadly, too many of us are still applying those lessons to our life because we haven't taken the time to unlearn bad habits and relearn the proper way to be a man. Even those of us who had fathers picked up some of these negative attributes by the men we referred to as "dad." So many of us had "fatherhood" incorrectly modeled to us and it translates in our relationships with our Heavenly Father and with the women in our lives.

Even the way we worship has been affected by our pride. Men today are afraid to expose themselves in worship just much as we are afraid to ask for help. So many of us have been raised with that "I can do it myself" mentality. It shows even when we call on GOD. Collectively, women approach the LORD with much more intimacy than men. They come with a "daddy's little girl" mindset and they don't struggle with casting their cares upon the GOD the Father. With arms outstretched and voices lifted high, women cry out to their Heavenly Father with more reverence and passion. Not worried with how they look, most women have no problem blocking out what others think of them. With a lot of us men, we'll throw up a fist for two seconds as if we're saying "hi" to one of our homeboys. We're too proud to cry out bitterly like Mordecai did before GOD delivered the Jews from a great slaughter in the book of Esther. In addition, many of us men lack the discipline to pray fervently like Daniel and Nehemiah. If we don't think this makes a difference in our society, all we have to do is look at the decline of leadership from men in the households, schools, and businesses. Prisons are filling up quickly by the day and this is no coincidence. The pride of many men has separated us from GOD and it is reflecting in many facets of our existence.

Getting back to the behavior of genuine worship is the only way men have a legitimate chance of making change happen in a broken world. It has always been GOD's intention to restore everything back to its rightful order. The issue is that there are not enough men taking this walk seriously. Grasping humility begins with a proper fear and reverence for the LORD. A man will never walk in his proper identity until he fully is in alignment with GOD. This means until he submits himself totally unto GOD, he will fall short in his marriage, he will fall short in his work, and he will fall short in his endeavors. Proverbs 15:33 states, "The fear of the LORD is the instruction of wisdom, and before honor is humility." I finally grasped the meaning of that verse in its entirety just a few years ago. I found that we have it all backwards.

By the time we become men, we all are jockeying for honor, respect, power, and success. Full of conceit, we make this our priority. Because of this, we find ourselves contending with each other in order to be the big dog on top. Instead of pausing for a moment to consider how we might try to please GOD, we vie for the approval and respect from men and women. Proverbs 15:33 actually gives us the order in how we should proceed. The scripture says, "...before honor is humility." In other words, until we humble ourselves we won't receive the true honor that comes from GOD. Otherwise we're striving for it in vain, which has been our pointless cycle since the beginning of time. Only GOD can give us the respect we desire from HIM and from man. Proverbs 3:3-4 ~ *"Let not mercy and truth forsake you; bind them around your neck, write them on the tablet of your heart and so find favor and high esteem in the sight of GOD and man."* The best form of humility is honoring others before yourself. When we men shed our selfish nature and begin putting the desires of GOD and others before ourselves, then we will see all of our relationships flourish, including the relationship we have with women.

Chapter 4:

The Patience of Ruth and Meekness of Boaz

I heard a renowned Christian rapper quote, "If you think being meek is weak, then try being meek for a week." How profound is that play on words? It's true though. Being meek is not easy and if more of us men knew how to balance the two, our relationships and marriages would be stronger. There are two husband and wife teams that I admire in the bible; one is in the Old Testament and the other is in the New Testament. In this chapter, I want to focus on the Old Testament relationship between husband and wife. I'm talking about the courtship of Ruth and Boaz. Though the book of Ruth is relatively short, there is so much that is being modeled for us in that story line if we allow the Holy Spirit to lead us in all understanding. For most of this book, the women have read my appeal to the men. I have challenged us to get our act together with many strong statements. However, in this chapter I want the women to pay close attention because for us to really strengthen the unity between us as men and women, both sides have to carry their weight.

Before we look at the attributes of Boaz, let's look at what the LORD was doing in the life of Ruth. When we're first introduced to the woman of GOD, she was amidst a tragic season accompanied by a huge famine in the whole land. She was a Moabite by ethnicity. In an unusual family situation, Ruth finds herself as one of three women whose husbands had died. She, her mother-in-law, and her sister-in-law all shared the same fate. Ruth's mother-in-law, Naomi was Jewish and heard that the LORD had returned grace to the children of Israel and provided them with food during the recession. The three women had clung together as family even beyond the deaths of their husbands. Naomi, saw no fit for her to remain in Moab where she and her husband dwelt prior to his passing. Ruth and her sister-in-law, Orpah, were married to Naomi's sons and had cared for Naomi after her loss. Nonetheless, when Naomi decided to head back to Judah, she told her daughter-in-laws to remain in Moab. Even against Naomi's reluctance and refute for her daughter-in-laws to remain, Ruth "clung" to Naomi as the Bible states. Orpah kissed Naomi goodbye to be never heard from again, but there was something deeper within Ruth evidenced by her response to her mother-in-law;

Ruth 1:16 ~ But Ruth said, "Entreat me not to leave you, or to turn back from following after you. For wherever you go, I will go; and wherever you lodge, I will lodge; your people will be my people and your GOD will be my GOD..."

Ruth's desire was on the LORD. Her people, the Moabites, did not serve GOD but rather several gods. Her ethnicity didn't matter to her. She knew the GOD of Israel was the only true GOD. Naomi could not persuade Ruth to leave her and the two of them came back to Bethlehem together. Because of her decision to follow GOD, the LORD had her best interest at heart. In a plan unbeknownst to her, the LORD had a beautiful destiny wrapped up for her because of her devotion towards HIM. In Ruth Chapter 2, we witness the introduction of Ruth to Boaz. Ladies, make a note; she was not looking for a husband. Understand that at the point of her evacuation from Moab, Ruth was giving up her culture, people, and even her language because of her love for GOD. Ruth was so focused on the task at hand, that she even takes a humiliating job as a gleaner in a field. This was all that was available for her, because employment was hard to find as much of the land was in a recession.

Naomi's faith in GOD had dwindled, but Ruth's faith remained strong in the LORD. What are the chances of her finding work on a field of a billionaire who happened to be a relative of Naomi's late husband? This was not a coincidence, though some would call it that. This was the LORD setting her up for breakthrough because of her obedience and trust in HIM. Against many odds, Ruth was hired to work on the field of a man of GOD who possessed wealth, honor and humility. She wasn't presuming or over-zealous in her approach to becoming the love of Boaz's life. As a matter of fact she was quiet and unpretentious, yet she worked diligently and the faithfulness she showed towards GOD and Naomi was reported to Boaz (Ruth 2: 10-13).

It is safe to say that Ruth desired a husband. Most women I know want to be loved by a man that makes them feel secure and protected. During this time in Ruth's life we can only imagine what she was feeling. She was a relatively young woman and the husband that she planned on spending her life with had passed away. Her hope, comfort, and security that she had planned on living under for a lifetime with this man was cut short by an unforeseen death. Added to that, she was by herself during a time of severe economic depression. In any event, Ruth's maturity and diligence in the LORD sets her apart from other women. Like other young women her age, she didn't chase after men for money or security. Look at Boaz's response to Ruth when he wakes up and finds her laying at as his feet;

Ruth 3:10-11~ "And he said, Blessed be you of the LORD: For you have showed more virtue in the latter end than at the beginning, inasmuch as you do not follow after young men whether they be rich or poor. And now, my daughter, fear not; I will do for you all that you require: For all the city of my people do know that you are virtuous."

Albeit, in those times there was a custom for when a woman's husband died. There was an option for the nearest male kinsmen or relative to *redeem* her as his own wife. Boaz, being a cousin of Naomi's husband put him in line to redeem Ruth who he found to be attractive inside and out. Nonetheless, Boaz being a man of honor and order, did not allow his emotions to preempt GOD's plan whether they favored him or not. According to scripture, there was another kinsman that was first in line to redeem Ruth. Though Ruth wanted to be with Boaz and Boaz wanted to be with Ruth, they both decided to leave it in the LORD's hand. Boaz told her that he would speak to the other relative before he could even claim her in his role as *"kinsmen-redeemer."* Ruth, being subjected to the laws and customs of that time, had to wait to find out if she would even be allowed to marry Boaz or end up the wife of another man. Even with his wealth and authority, Boaz digressed and gave way to LORD's decision on the matter.

When Boaz visited the relative to discuss his plans for Ruth and Naomi, he deferred to the relative out of respect to the custom. He didn't use his wealth or authority to sway his decision. The kinsman said he was unable to redeem Ruth because he did not want to forfeit his own inheritance. He then forgoes his rights as Kinsmen-Redeemer to Boaz. Boaz, after waiting on GOD to qualify his future with Ruth, buys all the possessions that were left of the deceased husband's and he purchased the right to marry Ruth.

One of the underlying themes in this love story is the virtue of patience needed for things to develop and the humility to trust in GOD while seeing it all through to the end. In the 21st century many of us have disregarded these attributes when it comes to relationships. We can learn a lot from these two. Their obedience in waiting on GOD allowed both of them to become ancestors in the direct lineage of Jesus. There is reward in our relationships when we wait on the LORD to qualify everything. In addition, there is a perfect peace (shalom) that comes with the marriage when the LORD is truly steering the helm of the relationship.

Have you ever met that married couple where when you walk in their house you get the feel like you're in "Pleasantville?" It seems so surreal that you would think it was fake. It almost feels like you're in an episode of the Cosby Show or Family Matters. I've met several pastors and their wives who exemplify this type of marriage lifestyle and it is not fake. It doesn't mean that they didn't have any uphill battles in their relationship at one time or another, but it means that their love and contentment for the LORD was definitely established in their marriage. This dichotomy only comes from two people who seek the LORD together with the patience and humility it takes to wait on GOD and to serve and honor each other.

In our humanity, it is so natural to move on an impulsive whim. We see something we like and 9 times out of 10 we'll go after it without doing the due diligence of thinking it over or giving it to GOD. We often do this in relationships, leaving GOD out in the process. Our attraction to another person can distract us from making GOD the priority. In these situations we usually take the authority in our own hands and the only time we want to give it to the LORD is when things become a mess. The truth is we don't like to wait. Men and women both want what they want, when they want it, and we want it done our way. Many of us do not have a clue what it genuinely means to wait on the LORD. It is not a feeling that comes over us that lets us know when it's right. Too many of us had a "feeling" in the past only to find out that was not the person we were looking for. Our emotions should not be our final authority on our decisions in any case, let alone relationships. The way we determine whether GOD's qualified a matter is through HIS word (scriptures), through the revelation of answered prayer, the multitude of witnesses (wise counsel of multiple people of GOD), and just seeing something come to pass that you have inquired about. Be mindful that sometimes when GOD is confirming a matter, it may take some time. Recall Abraham's servant in Genesis 24. These are a few of the many ways GOD lets us know HIS hands are in a matter.

However, if we don't take the time to seriously get to know GOD, there is no way of knowing how HE works. Knowing GOD means understanding that he doesn't always answer right away. It is understanding that sometimes we need to press into much prayer before he does qualify some things in our life. During the time of our waiting we should be praying, meditating and reading because those are major components through which GOD brings revelation. When Boaz heard Ruth's request for him to redeem her the night he woke up with her at his feet, he didn't immediately adhere to her proposition. She had already found favor in his eyes and he knew she was beautiful. Albeit, Boaz wanted to marry Ruth but had to wait because there was a custom that had to be followed before he married her. Boaz could have went based solely off his emotions and avoided the custom and possibly gotten away with it for the moment. If he had done that it would not have honored GOD.

Many Christians pull the trigger on life decisions without allowing the Creator of life to steady our aim on the right target. Instead of waiting on the right time, we often fire prematurely hitting the wrong target and messing up the best laid plans that GOD had set before us. Meekness and patience are two of many attributes that GOD smiles upon and it moves HIM to bless us when we put them into practice. Let us all make a declaration as we are reading this to clothe ourselves with meekness and patience. Meekness is the submissive response that we have towards GOD and his Word. It means that we give precedence to the principles HE set in place and we obey every directive with a gracious attitude. Patience means that we wait ungrudgingly on GOD to give us his decision on a matter. In the process of our patience we should be honoring GOD with worship, praise, and adoration. Ruth and Boaz did this and lived it out through application in their lives. Their obedience left a legacy of godliness in a generational line that would eventually produce our Savior, who is contending for us to do the same thing in our families.

Chapter 5:

Waiting on GOD: Containing the Sexual Urge

Men like sex; so much to the point that many of us have become desensitized to the principles of GOD regarding sex. Many of us Christians have treated GOD's guidelines regarding sex like an option instead of a commandment. We tend to ignore the scriptures that speak on sex and in many churches we treat the topic like its taboo; ultimately creating an elephant-in-the-room atmosphere and leaving a door open so sin may continue. Sadly, many young men come into the church with much of their worldly ways attached to them and there are not enough disciples holding them accountable. That's because many of the church leaders are struggling with the same issues that many of the new parishioners have when they come in fresh from the world.

The Apostle Paul spoke vehemently to the men of the church of Corinth about their roles in GOD's kingdom and he touched extensively on abstaining from fornication. Like the churches of today, the men of Corinth struggled with sexual immorality among the congregation. In chapters 5-7 of 1st Corinthians Paul begins to address those in the church who were having sex. Believers fall when there is no accountability present. The church overall has lacked accountability in this area because not enough men are bold enough to rebuke each other when another one falls. We've been so accustomed to celebrating one another when we "get some" that now we have no idea as to how we're supposed to call each other out for immoral sin. Much of the church has given way to diplomacy, which is robbing our men of correction. While the world continues to entice and seduce people heavily with the appeal of sex and the club scene, we remain anesthetized by complacency and lethargy. I am pleased when I see young men seeking GOD in their youth, but I admit I am troubled by the number of us still allured by the worldly lusts of sex.

A good number of men and women struggle with dating inside the church because they are used to operating out of a world's system of doing things when it comes to courtship as opposed to doing it GOD's way.

The applications of abstinence are not taught thoroughly in numerous churches. In this event, many go into relationships with no boundaries. There is an assumption that because we're Christian; because we attend church and love GOD, there will be no temptation that we would have to endure. It's quite the contraire. So many of us go into a relationship with our guards down spiritually and we discover that we become slaves to the flesh even in our supposed "Kingdom" dating relationships. In his letters of the book of Romans and Galatians, Paul expressed that the flesh wars against the Spirit causing us to do the things that we know are wrong. Paul's letters were addressing those who were new in Christ and his letters would eventually become guidelines for us to live by.

Because of the proscribed approach to teaching sexual morality in the churches, many men are oblivious to the discipline it takes to walk in the Spirit and abstain from the lusts of the flesh. Let us not be so immature where we blame the beauty of a woman for our struggles in the flesh, but let us also not be unguarded to where the beauty of a woman becomes our distraction. Men are drawn by the physical first. I wish I could say we were as in touch with our emotional and mental side, but that is not the case. We are creatures that have to thoroughly be taught how to bring our flesh and our thoughts under the subjection of Christ. Immoral sex in the sanctuary occurs more common than people think.

Allowing fornication into our courtship prior to marriage takes GOD out of the equation. A relationship with sin involved in it means that GOD is not present in it. Regrettably, we men put ourselves and our mates in precarious situations because we often press for the physical intimacy prematurely. There is no such thing as a "90-day" rule when it comes to dating in the Kingdom. As Christians, we should be free from sex until we say "I do" to our mates in front of witnesses before GOD. Men of GOD have to be the "principals" in the relationships that establish godliness. The moment we allow our flesh to rule in the relationship is when everything becomes unaligned spiritually. Had Adam been on top of his game, Eve would have been kept away from sin. Had David been strong in the Spirit he wouldn't have caused Bathsheba to sin along with him. If Solomon would have guarded his heart, he would not have been pulled away by the hearts of many women who led him into sin. I believe you all are getting the picture.

Premature sex in the sanctuary has caused so many broken relationships. In many churches, it has marred the perception of marriage amongst both young men and women. The conviction after a fall usually causes unmarried couples to move further away from each other rather than closer. What has happened is premarital sex has become so common that even the men and women of the church are numb to the sin. It has become acceptable and sadly the value of marriage and sex has depreciated. Christian men have further added to the damage by consenting to engage in such acts with charm and deceit. The issue of fornication is upheld by the fact that most men are not properly taught how to contain their fleshly desires. Some don't want to be taught because they would rather be satisfied by the sensation of the flesh rather than walk in obedience. Some men are just addicted to "feeding their flesh" and like most addicts, they are in denial that they have a problem.

Fleshly addictions can make Christian men appear

as evil men in the eyes of others who judge us. Those addictions make us out to be hypocrites. The trustworthiness that people desire to see in us becomes a rap sheet of faithlessness, disloyalty, and deceit. We tell people we're one thing but end up showing ourselves to be something different. We then lose our testimony to others because of it. When a man of GOD falls, the world is quick to judge. This is why the LORD reminds us "do not let your good be evil spoken of (Romans

14:16)." So, what does it really mean for a man to "walk in the Spirit" as Paul writes about in the book of Galatians? What are the strategies for taming our fleshly desires, so that we're not looking just like the rest of the world? In Paul's letters to the church of Galatians we see Paul use phrases like "crucify the flesh with its passions and desires", "walk in the Spirit", and "do not fulfill the lust of the flesh." For men, this is a challenge in more ways than one. Because the sexual appetite is one of the most covetous natures of man, it is one of the hardest to bring under control. However, just like any other difficult task, curbing the sexual urge takes discipline and it takes work.

A lot of us guys who like working out, go to the gym for several hours throughout the week to train and build muscle. We fail to realize that the physical mirrors the spiritual; being that we're all created by the Spirit of GOD. So that all can identify with this, I will use the analogy in the physical so we can understand the spiritual discipline it takes to walk according to GOD's word. When we begin to lift weights, run, crossfit, swim, or perform any other kind of exercise, our physical bodies begin to take on a different type of sculpted form.

Muscles begin to form in certain areas and the body becomes more attractive. Too many of us focus on the sculpting the outside and pay very little attention to the inward, which is far more important. I am talking about the Spirit; aka the inner man.

Just like the physical body, the Spiritual body needs exercise. The difference is that the spiritual is the one that determines our life time in eternity. The inner man is the one that lasts for an eternity. Depending on what we exercise in the Spirit and what we feed our Spirit, the outcome will have an effect on how strong or weak our inner man is. We exercise our faith by studying

GOD's word every day. Just like waking up every day and going to the gym takes a degree of discipline, so does studying GOD's word. Spiritual understanding takes time and it is the apparatus upon which we build our faith muscle. Romans 10:17 reminds us that "faith comes by hearing…" and we hear from GOD by reading his word. Secondly, we need a healthy prayer life. Prayer is the strengthening machine that we can apply to different parts of our inner man. However, repetitions are the key. In the same manner, a man who lifts weights knows that the more reps you do, the bigger and stronger you become. Well, in the spiritual, the more reps you do with reading GOD's word, meditating, praying, and fasting- the bigger and stronger your spirit becomes. Spiritual exercise is necessary so that you're able to contend against the flesh and the fleshly temptations like immoral sex, masturbation, pornography, and adultery. Paul reminded us in Galatians 5:17 that the flesh and spirit war with one another and too many men in this world are losing the battle with the flesh; including those who go to the gym.

Many men in this day and time struggle with

delineating between walking in the Spirit and walking in the flesh. The world has done a good job of subconsciously swaying the minds of men into compromise. Because of the commonality of sex, we have accepted it as a regular part of our society. Televisions shows display it, the internet hosts and markets it, songs beg for it, and we practice it whether we're married or not. Oblivious to what it means to be Spirit led, we walk according to our flesh throughout most of our day. With the majority of men who live in this world walking according to their fleshly desires, it's a wonder as to why GOD's grace has sustained us thus far. The media and industry know how to appeal to our fleshly appetites. If our inner man is weak, we will fall victim to those temptations that are blasted through our minds on the regular.

Our battle cry now should be one for the men of this world to become Spirit-led and transformed. The transformation process for a lot of men lately has been stalled in mid-metamorphosis because many of us keep one foot in Egypt and the other in Israel. In other words, we'll walk in godliness to a certain extent but continue to do the same thing the world does when it is fitting to us. It is as if we don't allow the transformation of GOD to fully take place in us. Who has ever heard of a caterpillar coming half way out of the cocoon being half butterfly, half caterpillar? It would be an odd picture wouldn't it? Part of him trying to fly and the other half of him grounded; still in the cocoon because it's not fully developed. That's why many of us hardly experience the true nature of GOD. We're grounded because we haven't fully let go of the things of this world when the LORD is trying to take us higher. Sexual promiscuity keeps so many of us from progressing into the men of GOD that the LORD desires for us to be. As we become the true definition of a Christian men, not just a title, we must shed off every desire of the flesh

and live fully as transformed men of

GOD.

Chapter 6:

The Aquila and Priscilla Paradigm:

How Do We Know Who's Right For Us?

Paul makes a suggestion to those who are single not to seek a wife or a husband (1st Corinthians 7:27). This does not sound encouraging to those of us who desire to be mates. Some would argue the point, "How are we supposed to find our mates if we don't look?" Some would even say that Paul's statements contradict earlier parts of the bible since Proverbs 18:22 states, "He who finds a wife, finds a good thing and obtains favor from the LORD." I confess, being a man who loves the idea of dating and marriage, it was tough for me to follow what Paul was conveying. It wasn't until I looked closer at the context of his letter that I understood in totality what Paul was preaching. Paul's pretext for his statement had to do with remaining focused on the LORD. Some of the members in the church of Corinth struggled with focusing on their relationship with the LORD because they were focused on intimacy with one another. Paul understood that if a man embarked on a mission to find a wife, it would distract him on his mission in seeking Christ.

Paul wasn't hating on marriage, nor was he against it. Paul understood the temptations that can pull men away from serving GOD to their fullest. Much like times today, the young men at Corinth were struggling in their devotion to GOD because they were distracted by the beauty of the women in the church. Many of them were trying to find mates and in their attempts, a plethora of them were falling into fornication. This is why Paul spends three chapters in 1st Corinthians (5-7) addressing the issues of fornication, dating, and marriage. Paul actually lived with, worked with, and travelled with a married couple who I consider the model husband and wife team of the early church.

Aquila and Priscilla were indeed a husband and wife team that represented a strong model of marriage. They worked together and their marriage was a radical dichotomy separate from what society was used to at that time. In a male-dominant society where men looked at their wives as property, Aquila and Priscilla walked their marriage out in congruency to what Paul preached in Ephesus. There, he charged the men to love their wives as

Christ loved the church (Ephesians 5:25). The couple is mentioned only 6 times in the Bible in four different books, but in those few passages they show how a marriage should look. They worked together in ministry (Acts 18:2-3), they ministered and reproved together (Acts 18:26), and they sacrificed their lives together for the greater good of the body of Christ (Romans 16:3-4). Priscilla was not Aquila's property. She was interdependent of her husband but rather epitomized her role as his partner in marriage and in ministry. Hardly ever apart from one another, Aquila and Priscilla served as missionaries with Paul on many of his journeys to build and establish churches. So how did they get here? How did this couple, Jewish- Christian converts exiled from Rome, end up becoming such prime examples for Christian couples?

First and foremost, Aquila and Priscilla's marriage was deeper than a romance. The relevance of their accounts in the bible was focused on their "togetherness" in ministry along with the objectives they were accomplishing in the Kingdom of God. As a unit, they achieved much together for the purposes of GOD. That is the true premise behind marriage. This is why GOD created marriage; for man and woman to live together for his glory. However, through the course of time, we have diminished the value and sanctity of marriage with our own regulations instead of following GOD's true intention for it. SO…. WHERE DOES GOD FIT INTO THE DATING EQUATION?

With Paul's take on marriage versus our own perception on dating, it is likely for us to become confused on how to find a mate. The Christian walk has never been easy in any aspect, including dating. Because we want to follow Christ, we find ourselves trying to determine whether matchmaking is a divine process, a matter of personal selection, or a combination of both. Biblically, we have examples but we have to determine how far we're willing to trust GOD according to what his word says. If we try to determine what role GOD plays in our relationships based on the examples we see around us, we can easily fool ourselves. "Christians" have the higher percentage of divorces when compared to those who consider themselves non-Christians. As mentioned earlier, I was a part of two congregations where I've seen pastors have to step down because of their inability to remain loyal. So when a relationship goes bad, does it mean that GOD wasn't the foundation of the marriage?

Our relationships with our mates should be Christ-centered and organic. When we study the context of the bible closely, we can see the contrast between relationships that were of divine process and those that were of man's selection minus GOD's intervention. An example of GOD's providence in two people coming together would be the account of Isaac and Rachel in Genesis 24. With the man (Isaac) absent from the equation, the LORD intervenes on behalf of the prayer of Abraham's servant who was sent to find Isaac a wife. Another would be the account of Ruth and Boaz. Though personal selection had some to do with their unity, ultimately it was the LORD's confirmation that granted their matrimony. When man or woman take the selection process into their own hands and leave GOD out, the relationship is prone to failure. King David on two accounts left GOD out of the equation. His first marriage ended up in divorce to Michal and his second was premised on adultery with Bathsheba. Solomon didn't consult the LORD in his relationships and because of it, his heart was carried away by many women. Sampson and Delilah ended up in disaster and death. The point of the matter is that the LORD should be present and the deciding factor in all of our relationships.

Just because we attend church with someone that we're attracted to, does not always mean that it is okay for us to make the move. There has to be a degree of patience on our parts and we have to learn how to wait on GOD to qualify it as Abraham's servant did (Genesis

24:21). GOD qualifying our relationship does not mean an angel will descend from the sky and tell us who our mate is or whether or not we've made the right decision. We have to stop looking for "signs" when it comes to relationships. Letting the LORD qualify your relationship means "staying quiet" and "being still" until he reveals himself through that peace in your heart.

Sometimes, in order for us to get clarity on a situation through GOD, we have to consecrate ourselves for a period of time. For instance, when we are in the midst of making a tough decision there should be a time where we separate ourselves from what we're dealing with and get before the LORD. Doing this allows us to receive divine clarity. Do you remember Moses on Mt. Sinai? He was in the midst of leading the nation of Israel out of captivity and into Canaan (the land of Promise). Nevertheless, Moses had to go before the LORD in the midst of chaos to get wisdom and understanding. The children of Israel were becoming restless, they were sinning continuously and the journey was tedious. So, for 40 days and 40 nights, Moses went before the LORD for directions. Both men and women alike, have to become like Moses when seeking GOD's answer to the relationships we entertain in our lives.

Even when the LORD qualifies our relationship, we still have a work to do. We don't just sail off into marital bliss. We must see marriage in the same light that we see salvation. Paul reminds us in Philippians 2:12 to "work out our salvation with fear and trembling." Like salvation, we have to work on our marriages and that work begins in the dating phase. The loyalty, trust, love, and consistency you develop in a marriage is built the moment you start courting your potential spouse. It doesn't start when you say "I do". It starts before then.

Mistakenly, many Christians take dating too lightly. As a matter of fact, many of us treat dating like most of the world does. We view it as a smorgasbord for one-night stands or temporary gratification with the person we like at the moment. Instead, we need to treat it more seriously. We should see it as the launching pad where maintenance is being done on both parties before they ascend into their kingdom identities together as a unit. When we are preparing for something sacred, we need to be treating the preparation process seriously. Christians need to see the dating process as preparation for marriage. No Christian should date "just for the hell of it." Surely enough, hell would be getting the pleasure out of that as the devil has pointed his finger and accused the church many years for our inconsistencies with loving each other properly.

When we think of the analogical depiction that we get of Christ and the church being compared as a husband and wife in Ephesians 5:22-33, we start to understand the serious nature of marriage. Throughout scripture, there are several references where JESUS is called the bridegroom and the people (of the church) are prompted to get ready for the "wedding". I often view preparation for that wedding much like the sanctification process that takes place in Exodus 19 prior to the LORD coming down to visit Moses and the children of Israel. The people were cleansing themselves and husbands were charged not to go near their wives.

They were getting ready for the presence of the LORD. In the dating phase of our relationships we should be sanctifying ourselves and helping each other prepare for the coming of the LORD. When the wedding day arrives, our vows that we say before the LORD and witnesses should only confirm that which we have already been doing with our mates prior to the wedding.

Finally, our GOD is infinite. If it is for us to be married, then we can expect our LORD to introduce us to our mates in many different ways. Some of us might meet our spouses in a Starbuck's line, in a grocery store, while we're walking our dogs, or taking out the trash. The LORD delights in surprising us through unexpected ways. Some of us may take the bold approach and walk right up to the woman who has caught our eye to begin a conversation. Others may inquire through a friend to be introduced. Whatever way we begin to walk into a relationship, let us remember to give Christ the final decision on the matter through much prayer and patience. Let's all practice discipline by putting our emotions to the back and allow GOD to qualify our next move as we remain silent and watching like Abraham's faithful servant did when Rachel became the wife of Isaac.

Chapter 7:

Restoring Eden: How Can Two Walk Together?

When the LORD created Adam, he created Eve to be his helpmate; and his helpmate alone. He didn't create Adam and Eve, Jacqueline, Tania, Tanisha, etc. We don't have to question GOD on everything to know his intentionality or reason for doing something. The model of marriage was created within Eden; one husband and one wife. Sometimes, all we have to do is go back to moments of creation to find his purpose behind certain affairs. I opened up speaking on the destruction of Shalom in the Garden of Eden in Chapter 1. The perfect peace that was destroyed in Eden had a direct effect on our relationship with GOD and with our mates. Since that time, our existence here on earth has been about the LORD trying to redeem us to be HIS again. It's been about ushering a new regime of perfect peace starting with the relationship that we have with GOD. It is through Christ that we can attain that. When our walk with the LORD is precise, our relationships with our mates will be as well. The catch is that both parties have to be walking with Christ.

The LORD poses the question to the children of Israel through the prophet Amos, "Can two walk together unless they agree?" (Amos 3:3). The answer to that is two people can't walk together for long if they don't agree. The main ingredient to making our relationships work with the opposite sex is a consistent and daily walk with the LORD. In a relationship, the couple's walk should resemble, what I call, "a pyramid model." The man and woman are on a parallel line standing on opposite ends. GOD is placed high above and directly in the middle of the line. As the man and woman continue to seek GOD as individuals and relationally, they both begin to ascend on separate lines which ultimately brings them closer to GOD and each other.

"Pyramid Model" of man and woman walking with Christ.

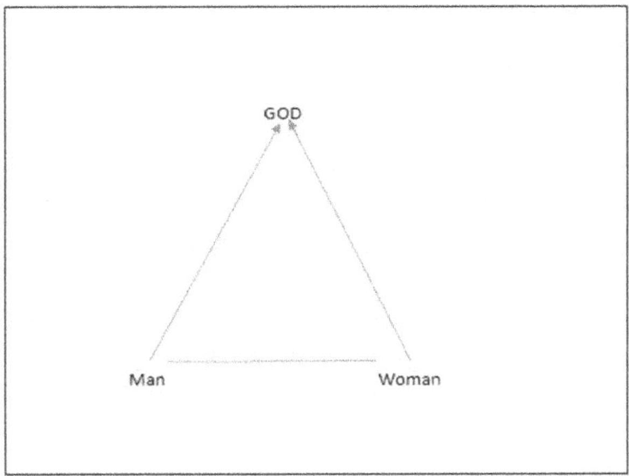

Let's put dating and marriage in its proper context once and for all. Yes, the LORD did create man and woman to be together. However, he created them to be together under certain principles and guidelines that we are supposed to obey. There is nothing wrong for a man and a woman to meet in the house of GOD. For those of us who are skeptical of dating within the church because of prior bad experiences, do not be discouraged. What better place to meet your potential spouse? Paul writes in 2nd Corinthians 6:14 for us "not to be unequally yoked with unbelievers." Developing monogamous relationships in the church with our potential spouses is a good thing. We just have to make sure we are obedient and follow his commandments regarding dating, marriage, and sex. If we're honest with ourselves, the bad experiences that we have in church happen because we are out of alignment with GOD's word. We put ourselves in predicaments and then get mad at the person for letting us down. Nonetheless, as believers we shouldn't be in the clubs, strip clubs, or on the corner trying to pick up our future wives or husbands. The kingdom of GOD is a great place for an organic, long-term relationship to begin, whether it is through a missions trip, attending the same church, serving on the same ministries, or meeting through church revival collaborations. The LORD delights in bringing couples together and establishing relationships. Why wouldn't he? He created us and wired us for intimacy and to be in relationships. However, it is not good for us to put any relationship before GOD. That becomes idolatry. Even in the pursuit of wooing our mates, there are confines we must remain within. These confines are not to hold us captive, but to make sure we don't fall in to sin which will surely hold us captive.

The man and woman must first stand in agreement to walk in righteousness in order for the LORD to be glorified in the relationship. There are too many Christians playing house; shacking up, sleeping in the same bed, playing the wife or husband without vows are ways we can dishonor the LORD and the relationship. I've seen way too many couples end their relationship in the dating process because they overstepped boundaries in the courtship phase that shouldn't have been crossed until they were married. When Christian men and women begin to take dating seriously, then we'll see stronger marriages develop corporately among all churches. Too many adult Christians compromise non- negotiables in the dating stage and they end up ruining what could be a beautiful union because they preempt the LORD. GOD then takes his hands off of the relationship because the couple have decided to try to do things according to their own will and in their own time.

In order to bring dating and marriage back into what GOD intended for it to be, we need to start teaching and modeling proper aspects of dating and marriage to our young boys and girls. This starts with the church body.

Pastors, bishops and deacons have to speak on the topic instead of shying away from it. Diplomacy and subtlety are not beneficial to the Christian faith when it comes to teaching on dating and marriage. With so many wrong innuendoes being pumped through television and the radio, the younger generations are subconsciously applying wrong moralities to their relationships and causing each other to fall and stumble along the way as they compromise their walk with CHRIST.

I use the phrase "It's all in how you see it" a lot. In general, women and men perceive marriage differently. Many women see it as the day they have been waiting for their whole life, while men communally struggle with the ball & chain perception. Many men, including Christian men view marriage as a form of bondage or limitation; scared to commit to, what may become according to their eyes, a life sentence of torture and boredom. This presents the issue of discontentment in far too many marriages. When a marriage loses its luster it's usually because one or both of the members of the relationship have taken their eyes off of what matters. Relationships that are Christ-centered mean that both the man and the woman are walking with their eyes on the savior because they understand that their marriage is deeper than just a romance. Romance is definitely needed to keep the relationship joyous and moving forward, but the true foundation of a marriage's success and duration is the collaborative objective of what the couple is trying to obtain during their time together. Those who perceive their marriage as a life- time ministry focused on representing the kingdom of GOD know how to endure the hardships together as they walk out the mission GOD had laid out for them.

Men and women who understand each other's mission in Christ, stand strong with each other even when the times get rough. They don't abandon each other when arguments arrive, nor do they look for solace in another relationship. Both the man and the woman understand when they both said "I do", it was underneath a Christ covenant.

The Effervescence of Ephesians 5

In Ephesians 5, the Apostle Paul once again addresses the issues of fornication, marriage, and idolatry as he did in 1st and 2nd Corinthians. Paul talks about "walking" in three different capacities. In Ephesians 5:1-7 he talks about walking in love (v2 - *and walk in love, as Christ also has loved us and given Himself for us,..*) ; in Ephesians 5: 8-14 he instructs us through the Holy Spirit to walk as children of light (*v8- For you were once in darkness, but now you are light in the LORD. Walk as children of light*), and in Ephesians

5:15-21 he charges us to walk in wisdom (*v15- See then that you walk circumspectly, not as fools but as wise*). He hit on these three areas while expounding to the believer to have no part with fornication, becoming drunk, or idolatry. He addressed these right before closing out the letter with instructions to make sure our marriages emulate the marriage between Christ and the church.

Paul stressed us "walking" together in Christ

because he understood that our relationship with Christ was indeed a life-long walk. The discipline of walking together takes even more effort when we are married. As the apostle begins to address the issue of marriage he uses the word "submit" twice in verses 21 and 22. In verse 21 we are told to "submit to one another." In verse

22, Paul tells wives to submit to their husbands but very few of us, even those of us in the Christian faith, understand what submission means. In Paul's use of the word it means "support". The man has a "*mission*" in Christ and the woman comes *underneath* the man to support his mission, hence the prefix "sub" meaning underneath. Paul corroborates this in verse 23 which states, "For the husband is the head of the wife as Christ is head of the church; and he is the *Savior* of the body."

As men, we have missed that role in our relationships with our women. The LORD is charging us to be *saviors* in our relationships. Verse 25 of Ephesians 5 says that "Christ loved the church and gave himself for her", which signifies his death for all of mankind. The LORD is charging us men to love our wives in such a way, that we would lay down our life for her. When we enter into marriage with our mates we have to undertake the meaning of "one flesh" to heart. It's not just a phrase that the LORD threw together for us to forget. It was for us to apply. None of us would hurt our own bodies as the word reminds us verse 28 and 29. Instead we nourish and cherish our own bodies, as many of us do when we go into the gym to train. Likewise, as Christians, we must change the familiarity and the transverse monotony that our society has caused marriage to be viewed as.

We've become desensitized to the fact that marriage is not honored as the sacred pledge that was supposed to link man and women for a lifetime.

Definitively, in our Christian walk we can be examples to others in how we obey Christ and in how we treat our women. A spiritual reconciliation is needed between our men and women overall. A new humility among us men is necessary; a humility that speaks to us first making a new covenant with our LORD that we are going to be men of righteousness, men of one wife as we're commanded to be in 1st Timothy 3. We also have to wake up from the apathetic anesthesia that we have been asleep under for so many years; treating our relationships with women as second rate options. For those of us who are calling ourselves Christians, GOD is calling for us to be different. HE is waiting for us to be proactive in changing the world...but not by title or by what we call ourselves. Instead, the LORD wants us to change the world by action. If we're so fortunate to have a mate in the course of our GOD given mission, let us honor one another according to word of GOD and not by the world's standards. As we are instructed in James 1:22, let us all strive to be doers of the WORD, and not hearers only.

CHAPTER 8:

The Institution of Marriage

Columnist John Calvin Thomas, also known as "Cal" Thomas, made an interesting remark concerning marriage. He said, "More damage is being done to the institution of marriage by heterosexuals who are divorcing than by homosexuals attempting to get married." I thought it was a profound statement and as I began to think about it more, I did not find it strange at all that GOD would allow the many states in our country to begin constitutionalizing gay marriages. The church has not done a good job of honoring the covenant of marriage, so how can we expect the world to honor it?

In Matthew 19:1-12, Jesus gives an awesome tutorial on the institution of marriage and the history of divorce; 1 When Jesus had finished saying these things, he left Galilee and went into the region of Judea to the other side of the Jordan. 2 Large crowds followed him, and he healed them there. 3 Some Pharisees came to him to test him. They asked, "Is it lawful for a man to divorce his wife for any and every reason?" 4 "Haven't you read," he replied, "that at the beginning the Creator

'made them male and female,' 5 and said, 'For this reason a man will leave his father and mother and be united to his wife, and the two will become one flesh' ? 6 So they are no longer two, but one. Therefore what God has joined together, let man not separate." 7 "Why then," they asked, "did Moses command that a man give his wife a certificate of divorce and send her away?" 8 Jesus replied, "Moses permitted you to divorce your wives because your hearts were hard. But it was not this way from the beginning. 9 I tell you that anyone who divorces his wife, except for marital unfaithfulness, and marries another woman commits adultery." 10 The disciples said to him, "If this is the situation between a husband and wife, it is better not to marry." 11 Jesus replied, "Not everyone can accept this word, but only those to whom it has been given. 12 For some are eunuchs because they were born that way; others were made that way by men; and others have renounced marriage because of the kingdom of heaven. The one who can accept this should accept it."

Yet, we disregard this scripture. Why? Because of the hardness of our hearts. In my adult life, I've witnessed a handful of pastors and assistant pastors leave their wives; some for other women. This has become commonplace unfortunately. The value of marriage has been depreciated by mankind simply because we don't value our women the way GOD'S word commands us to. Ephesians 5:22-25 tells us, "22 Wives, submit yourselves unto your own husbands, as unto the LORD. 23 For the husband is the head of wife, even as Christ is the head of the church; and he is the savior of the body. 24 Therefore as the church is subject unto Christ, so let the wives be to their own husbands in everything 25 Husbands, love your wives, even as Christ also loved the church.

The part that many of us men overlook in that scripture is that GOD is calling us to be saviors in our relationships with our wives (verse 23). Men, we being the head of our wives does not mean we own them. Conversely, it means that we are to be the front line of our household and that we would give our lives for our wives. Exactly!!...the same way Christ gave his life for us, which is how he became our savior and sacrifice, so we could live forever. Unfortunately, our selfish nature has many of us failing to give of ourselves, hence the many failed marriages among us. We have not learned how to love as Christ loved.

In addition, because many of us are not stable in our relationships with the LORD, there is no way we can possibly be in a proper relationship with our wives. Many of the marriages in the church are built upon weak foundations as well as many marriages outside of the body of Christ. Now, because of the devalued perception of marriage by us collectively, we have allowed what once was a holy covenant between man and woman to become a perverted edict that allows same sex marriages. Make no mistake; GOD is not pleased. However, before we can even address the issues of the iniquitous same-sex marriage event happening in our world, we have to fix our marriages within our churches. Our examples of marriage as Christians to the world really hasn't been much of an act to follow. We become discontent in our marriages and we begin treating our wives less than the equals that GOD created them to be. We mistake the term “being the head” as meaning ownership instead of leadership.

Many of us become discontent with our wives because we have not learned how to be content with our lives. Discontentment stems from pride and men have been known to wrestle with this attribute from birth; some of us because of the way were conditioned. So many renowned men of the bible struggled with contentment, which is why so many of their marriages failed. Men like Abraham, Jacob, Sampson, David, and Solomon all loved GOD but struggled with contentment in their respective marriages. All of these men either took concubines or had sexual relations outside of the proper context of marriage with other women. Some even divorced their first wives and took on other wives. These issues have persisted well into the 21st Century.

Contrary to popular belief, GOD never intended for man to have more than one wife and as Jesus told us in Matthew 19, divorce was given to us by GOD the Father. Just because we see multiple men in the bible with multiple wives did not mean it was okay. GOD’s grace and mercy covered mankind despite their transgressions just like he didn't kill all of us who had sex outside of marriage. It doesn't mean fornication is allowed. Yet, our discontentment leads many of us out of our current relationships and in some cases it leads us in search for another. On the same note, our discontentment has left many of us broken.

A broken man or a broken woman entering into a relationship means there will be an unstable foundation, henceforth a shaky marriage. Until men and women learn how to love GOD with an undying, consistent devotion, we won't understand the value of relationships. GOD is the source of our creation, which makes him also the source of our relationships. Any relationship not built properly on the principles of GOD's word will not stand. This has been the premise behind many of the relationships in the church as of lately. We have not valued the principles of marriage, so we have failed to teach the principles to our young men and women.

Cal Thomas' remarks should challenge us who value marriage under GOD's proper covenant to re-examine our relationships with our wives. Many Christian men and women have ignored the ideologies of marriage presented by Paul in 1st Corinthians chapters 5-7. Paul warns couples to not defraud one another. In other words, do your husband and wife duties, particularly in the romance category. Paul even advises for the husband and wife teams to only be apart for a short time due to fasting and prayer, but then to come back together quickly so the devil doesn't get the opportunity to come in fill each spouse's thoughts with impurities. Overtime, many of us neglect to keep the fire burning in our relationships with our significant others, which caters to discontentment. If we step back and examine our "fair-weather" relationship with The LORD, we will probably see our marriages reflect that same "fair- weather" dichotomy with our spouses. Nonetheless, we have given way to satan as a whole. He has entered into many of our relationships and spoiled them to the point of divorce. We allowed it because our hearts were not perfect with the LORD.

Marriage is not easy. No one said it would be. However, as individuals, we have to learn that we are not our own...in any case. We have to give of ourselves to GOD and to our other half when it comes to the topic of relationships. To save the institution of marriage we need to take note of a popular Matt Redman song and get back to the "Heart of Worship." When both spouses' hearts are aligned in proper worship towards GOD in fullness and consistency, they will experience the outpouring of GOD's love through each other because GOD is at the center. It is then that contentment remains permanent and the delusional feeling of discontentment becomes obsolete. Amen.

ABOUT THE AUTHOR

Author and Christian Relationship coach, Chayil Champion is the author of multiple books that speak to relationships and perseverance. After receiving Christ as his personal savior at the University of Miami, Champion continued to build upon his Christian foundation by joining Athletes-in-Action (AIA) and Fellowship of Christian Athletes (FCA). It was through these organizations that Champion grew in the LORD while competing as a two-sport athlete in football and track.

Champion is also an educator, spending over 12 years in education as an English Teacher, Football coach and Vice Principal before being called to full-time ministry. Champion studied and advanced in ministry under the teachings of Pastor Russel Johnson, Tom Mullins and Pastor Toure' Roberts. Champion has served in ministry for over 15 years and was co-founder of 5,000 Fathers ministry for men.

Now, as Champion continues to embark career as an author and his apostolic call to leadership, he aims to restore hope to the broken and oppressed with the message of Jesus Christ through teaching and writing. Champion currently resides in Santa Monica, CA where he serves in multiple outreach ministries that are designed to restore those suffering from poverty, homelessness, and addiction.

More Books by Chayil Champion:

Affiliated

Goin' Pro

Exiting The Wilderness: GOD's Plan for us to Repent, Conquer, and Prosper

You can catch up with Chayil on his website:

www.the brokenpulpit.com

www.ingramcontent.com/pod-product-compliance
Lightning Source LLC
Chambersburg PA
CBHW071816020426
42331CB00007B/1497

9780692637302